Chinese Painting

Chinese Painting

Mario Bussagli

Paul Hamlyn

LONDON · NEW YORK · SYDNEY · TORONTO

Translated by Henry Vidon from the Italian original

La Pittura Cinese

© *1966 Fratelli Fabbri Editori, Milan*

This edition © 1969
The Hamlyn Publishing Group Limited
Hamlyn House,
The Centre, Feltham,
Middlesex

Text filmset in Great Britain by Yendall & Co. Ltd,
London

Printed in Italy by Fratelli Fabbri Editori,
Milan

Outside Europe, there is no livelier, richer or more technically accomplished tradition of painting than that of China.

Chinese painting has for a long time attracted attention in the West, not continuously, perhaps, and particularly at first only to be instinctively but wrongly compared with Western standards of technique and composition.

Marco Polo, astonished observer of Cathay, the China of the Mongols, tells us nothing about the great Chinese painters then living, unlike Father Matteo Ricci (1552-1610) who, in January 1601, arrived at the court of Peking as the first Catholic missionary. Yet, while praising Chinese artists for their extraordinary natural talent, Ricci declared that they could not compete with Europeans because 'they do not know how to paint in oils or give shadows to what they depict'.

For generations, the main charge against Chinese painters, and those of other Asian schools as well, was

1. Giuseppe Castiglione (Lang Shih-ning) (1698-1768).
*The Ambassadors of the Kazak Kirghiz presenting Two
Horses to the Emperor Ch'ien-lung* (detail). Ch'ien-lung
period. Musée Guimet, Paris.

2. Giuseppe Castiglione (Lang Shih-ning) (1698-1768).
*The Ambassadors of the Kazak Kirghiz presenting Two
Horses to the Emperor Ch'ien-lung* (detail). Ch'ien-lung
period. Musée Guimet, Paris.

9

1.   Giuseppe Castiglione (Lang Shih-ning) (1698-1768). *The Ambassadors of the Kazak Kirghiz presenting Two Horses to the Emperor Ch'ien-lung* (detail). Ch'ien-lung period. Musée Guimet, Paris.

2.   Giuseppe Castiglione (Lang Shih-ning) (1698-1768). *The Ambassadors of the Kazak Kirghiz presenting Two Horses to the Emperor Ch'ien-lung* (detail). Ch'ien-lung period. Musée Guimet, Paris.

In these two pictures the Milanese painter shows his ability as a portraitist and applies Western rules of perspective to the architecture.

3.   *Nighur Princess offering a Gift.* Votive picture on canvas dated AD.983. From Tun-huang. P. Pelliot Collection, Musée Guimet, Paris.

3.   *Nighur Princess offering a Gift.* Votive picture on canvas dated AD 983. From Tun-huang. P. Pelliot Collection, Musée Guimet, Paris. An example of Chinese influenced central Asiatic painting. Note how the figures of the women dominate the featureless room but without any psychological implication.

4.   *Horseman and Groom.* Painting on paper from Tun-huang. 8th century. Musée Guimet, Paris. The central Asiatic taste is clearly seen in the figures of the horses and the sketchy background.

4.   *Horseman and Groom.* Painting on paper from Tun-huang. 8th century. Musée Guimet, Paris.

that they did not know how to use scientific perspective. Critics thus ignored the fact that there were other ways, equally valid if less realistic, of showing perspective.

During the 17th and 18th centuries, contacts between Europe and China intensified progressively, and a number of missionary priests at the imperial court, mostly Italian or French, who happened to be painters as well, tried to spread Western technique and Western sensibility. Nobles, literati, senior officials, even the emperor himself showed interest in the realism obtainable by the Western handling of perspective. To satisfy their curiosity, a certain Father Buglio wrote a treatise on the subject in Chinese. But its readers clung to their belief that scientific perspective was only an exotic novelty. There were too many differences between European and Chinese painting to allow the treatise a more profound effect.

Typical of Chinese thinking were the views expressed by Wu Li (1632-1715). For this famous critic and good connoisseur of European painting, the West sought too much to render 'the external appearance and relief of forms', and he rebuked Westerners for exaggerated use of light and shade in their continual striving after effect in perspective and chiaroscuro.

To some extent, perhaps, these views were shared by Lang Shih-ning as he came to be called—Father Giuseppe Castiglione, the distinguished Milanese priest-painter who laboured in China from 1715 to

1768. The Emperor Ch'ien-lung deemed him the leading portrait-painter. Yet the Italian admired Chinese pictures for their rare refinement and power of expression. So much so, in fact, that he set out wholeheartedly to reconcile the opposing tendencies of East and West. He finally adopted a technique that was more Chinese than European. Moreover, his grasp of Chinese technique won him the reputation, which he still enjoys even among local critics, of being one of the great Chinese masters.

From what we have discussed so far, it is evident that, looked at with too Western an eye, Chinese paintings yield neither their beauty nor their secrets. Apart from the mania for *chinoiseries* and the admiration displayed throughout the 18th century for the minute perfection and exotic curiosity of Chinese craftsmanship, we have to jump to the second half of the Victorian era and slightly beyond for the first signs of genuine scientific interest in Chinese paintings. And that stemmed chiefly from the interest taken in Japanese prints, those beautiful creations that played no small part in the profound change in painting which occupied the European art world in the second half of the 19th century. Yet, even then, it could not be said that the West had forced itself to a proper appreciation of the immense heritage of art— and poetry—offered by Chinese painting. Beyond the restricted circle of specialists, that art remained almost unknown or, at best, appreciated by people whose hazy if not erroneous ideas stemmed from an un-avowed taste for the exotic. When all is said and done, Chinese painting is still often seen with Western eyes and still regarded as some sort of whimsical negation of our Western standards.

The misconception to which this approach gave rise has been accentuated by the fact that the first notable Western scholars echoed Japanese evaluations and relied on the latest Chinese critical texts. Consequently they applied traditional methods of evaluation to paintings and schools which, to be judged properly, should first have been accurately dated, so as to set them firmly into the period when they were created.

It is not long since we have become aware of this error. Osvald Sirèn admitted it openly and in 1958 brought out a completely rewritten edition of his colossal work on Chinese painting. That he should have undertaken such a task shows how determined this great scholar was to understand and judge accurately the aesthetic aims of a large number of artists.

And yet, despite all the difficulties in forming judgments and the need for background knowledge if one is to understand it clearly, Chinese painting is not as foreign to the Western world as it might seem. Bernard Berenson pointed out that occasionally the spirit of Chinese painting has a counterpart in our own, in the Sienese school of the 14th century and the first decades of the 15th, caused by the emotional and mystical drive of the Sienese people. Now, Berenson was thinking of a spiritual affinity rather than an historical connection, but it is not beyond the bounds of possibility that paintings of the Sung or very early Yüan could have suggested to Simone Martini something more than the dimensions of his great fresco in the Palazzo Pubblico of Siena representing Guidoriccio da Fogliano at the siege of Montemassi. The very treatment of the landscape, perhaps, of the palisade and of the flags and lances betrays here the presence of an army which we cannot see. Leaving aside the greatly different spirit that animated Simone's work—a clear expression of medieval Italian sensibility—the fact remains that the proportions of the fresco correspond to those of a Chinese hand scroll, the height being one third of the width. Moreover, details correspond and, yet another factor to point to imitation, Simone works them out just as Chinese artists would have done. To see the likelihood of such a derivation one need only compare Simone's fresco with the scroll by Chao Po-chü in the Boston Museum of Fine Arts. (Chao Po-chü was a Sung painter of imperial blood active about the middle of the 12th century.)

I do not intend now to reopen the complex, badly formulated and hastily resolved question of a relationship between the Sienese school and Far Eastern art. Nor do I wish to re-examine that other, more likely hypothesis—the influence of Chinese iconography on

5. Chao Mêng-fu (1254-1322) (attribution uncertain).
Picture of Wang-ch'uan. Copy of the landscape by Wang Wei.
Yüan dynasty. British Museum, London.

6. Chu Tuan (active 1506-1521). *River Landscape.*
Wu Tsung period. National Museum, Stockholm.

6

7. Chu Jui (attributed). Detail of a scroll illustrating
the poem of Su Tung-p'o, *The Red Rocky Precipice*.
National Palace and Central Museum Collections, Taichung
(Taiwan).

5.   Chao Mêng-fu (1254-1322) (attribution uncertain). *Picture of Wang-ch'uan.* Copy of the landscape by Wang Wei. Yüan dynasty. British Museum, London. Done for the purposes of study, this is a copy of a famous work by a painter already master of style but independent as regards the content.

6.   Chu Tuan (active 1506-1521). *River Landscape.* Wu Tsung period. National Museum, Stockholm. A fine evocative example of vertical composition with rocks, houses, trees, waterfalls and human beings in a clearly Chinese landscape.

7.   Chu Jui (attributed). Detail of a scroll illustrating the poem of Su Tung-p'o, *The Red Rocky Precipice.* National Palace and Central Museum Collections, Taichung (Taiwan). The overhanging effect of the rocks above the waters of the river is rendered from a viewpoint which makes good use of the mist, the clumps of vegetation and the vertical erosion.

8.   Ma Lin (*c.* 1220) (attributed). *Birds and Thorn Blossom.* Sung dynasty. National Museum, Tokyo. Although only a small detail in a lively landscape, the colours of this vignette suggest a mood. Hanging scroll in ink and colour on silk.

8. Ma Lin (*c.* 1220) (attributed). *Birds and Thorn Blossom.*
Sung dynasty. National Museum, Tokyo.

medieval European art. All I want to say is that the possibility of an East-West link is confirmed by other landscape details in works by Simone Martini.

Well attested commercial and cultural relations between Europe and the Far East from the mid 13th to the mid 14th centuries make the possibility of such a link seem all the more acceptable. Chinese art may well have suggested this or that exotic detail to the great Sienese painter. It may well have influenced his approach to painting and that of other Italians too, offering them something new by way of composition, iconography and even style.

The hypothesis is difficult to substantiate and for many difficult to accept. But even if it were shown to be false, there would still remain that world of painting so rich, refined and varied, a peerless interpreter of moods, landscapes and the tiniest details in nature, a world that tempts us to make the effort necessary to understand it.

The effort is well worthwhile, and I have written these pages with the precise object of helping you draw as close as you can to that world and its delights.

In the Chinese scale of aesthetic values top priority was given to calligraphy, painting, poetry and music. Partly because the materials employed were of small value and the things created heavy, architecture and sculpture were considered work for workmen. And the same applies to the minor arts where patient crafts-manship precluded immediacy of expression, the one exception being ceramics although they did not assume importance until later.

Calligraphy, painting and poetry are closely linked. The Chinese world of culture reflects a very special sort of society, one in which the 'literate man' is both painter and poet besides scholar and philosopher. His brush serves equally to give written form to his thoughts and pictorial form to his fantasies and moods. For the Chinese, writing is a sort of 'painting of thoughts'. The characters used to express ideas soon turn into 'ink games'. They have a rhythm of their own, independent of their meaning, which allows them to be appreciated as abstract drawings.

Chinese painting, therefore, is based on calligraphy, and it can be considered an emanation of that art. This explains why black ink was preferred to colour, and the importance assumed by the brush-stroke and the line. '*Le style est l'homme même*' ('style is the man himself'), we say in Europe. In China, it is more a case of a man's being reflected in his brush. For an instrument so fundamental in Chinese culture, it was only logical that a whole technique of manufacture and use should have come into being and evolved step by step with the passage of time. The brush was already known in the Chou dynasty (1027-256 BC). At first it probably did not differ greatly from that which we use for water-colours. Towards the beginning of the Christian era, however, the greater importance assumed by calligraphy led to its being modified.

A new pictorial technique, still in use today, had grown up alongside painting and drawing, in which relief or shadow is shown by a broadening of the brush-stroke and an increase or decrease of its density. By the 8th century AD the 'calligraphic' style was in general use, and 'dry' brushes *(kan-pi)* and 'wet' brushes *(shui-pi)* had been evolved, the latter being capable of absorbing and carrying more ink. Then the handles of the brushes were modified, and so were the hairs, those of a variety of animals being used and in varying lengths. Thus there developed an infinite range of brushes adapted for every need, short and long, thick and thin, but all in one of two categories, hard or soft. Naturally there were specialists in brush-making, some of whom became famous.

Like the brush, Chinese ink and ink-pots are also important. From them come the nature and consistency of the brush-stroke, factors which, among other things, help us establish dates and names that would otherwise be impossible to determine.

It was in the 8th century also that the taste for monochrome landscapes began to spread. Later on, these brush and ink pictures came to be considered the highest achievement of Far Eastern painting. The artist relied on the intensity and harmony of his brush-strokes to express and synthesise the inner meaning of nature, to act as a substitute for the effects of colour and to obtain the illusion of distance by gradually suppressing detail. Speaking of one of the 'Four Great

9. Painting on a prepared terracotta tile. From a tomb
near Lo-yang. 3rd century AD. Museum of Fine Arts, Boston.

10. Painting on a prepared terracotta tile (detail of a triangular tile). From a tomb near Lo-yang. 3rd century AD. Museum of Fine Arts, Boston.

9.   Painting on a prepared terracotta tile. From a tomb near Lo-yang. 3rd century AD. Museum of Fine Arts, Boston. An effective example of true stylistic harmony.

10.   Painting on a prepared terracotta tile (detail of a triangular tile). From a tomb near Lo-yang. 3rd century AD. Museum of Fine Arts, Boston. Note in this example too how the design gives the picture its value and how the colour complements the general effect.

11.   Ku K'ai-chih (*c.* 344-*c.* 406). *Admonitions of the Instructress to the Court Ladies* (detail). Copy of the T'ang dynasty. British Museum, London. These truly noble and refined figures, standing out between the moralising texts, seem to be holding a pose.

12.   Ku K'ai-chih (*c.* 344-*c.* 406). *Admonitions of the Instructress to the Court Ladies* (detail). British Museum, London. The faces are only apparently expressionless. In them and in the slender light bodies there is reflected the painter's character. With delicate brush-strokes, he succeeds in revealing their minds.

11. Ku K'ai-chih (*c.* 344-*c.* 406). *Admonitions of the Instructress to the Court Ladies* (detail). Copy of the T'ang dynasty. British Museum, London.

女史司箴敢告庶姬

聖不飾或愆禮正斧之漆之兄念行

12. Ku K'ai-chih (*c.* 344-*c.* 406). *Admonitions of the Instructress to the Court Ladies* (detail). British Museum, London.

Masters', Wu Chên (1280-c. 1354), Wu Li, that strange 18th-century painter, said, 'His pen contains all five colours.' His tribute was an allusion to Wu Chên's ability to obtain effects in ink instead of using coloured pigments, which shows the importance of good tools to painters, especially to calligraphers.

As for poetry, frequent accompaniment to a picture, its connection with painting was clearly stated by the 9th-century critic, Chang Yen-yüan: 'What could not be expressed in poetry was expressed in painting, and what could not be expressed in painting was expressed in poetry.' Refined Chinese appreciated a poem all the more when it was written out carefully in well formed characters, and with this continual interdependence calligraphy, painting and poetry evolved together. This may also explain why, throughout Chinese figurative art, there was a continual preference for certain themes and the symbolic values connected with them. At the same time fixed standards of judgment came to be established, so that a critical standpoint was laid down which in its turn affected the painting of the time.

The painting we are discussing is the great court genre cultivated by emperors and poets, officials and artists, literati and monks. It is done on silk or paper, used sometimes for the decoration of fans as well, and intended for deep, intimate contemplation. But there was another kind, the great murals, especially the Buddhist type, the decorative compositions and sacred pictures, often executed on canvas but sometimes on silk as well. These paintings belong to an entirely different class, a genre nearer to the sensibility diffused throughout Asia by the spiritual radiance of Buddhism, nearer still to that which animates the sacred art of the West although remaining indisputably Chinese. Often linked with the minutely descriptive directions of foreign texts and the rules of iconography codified in Indian treatises on sacred pictures, it has a very different story. Full of problems neatly solved, its object is to narrate and edify. On the human image and on the anthropomorphic image of divine beings, it confers supreme importance. In brief, it is as far removed as could be from the dreams, the aspirations and the fantasies of the court painters. It was seldom appreciated by the local critics, and was often considered mere craftsmanship, all the more so on account of its cavalier treatment of line and brushstroke. The figures are always outlined and treated, if at all, with a variety of colours to obtain the effect of chiaroscuro. In some cases the effect was striking and very 'modern'. And this is due not so much to the summary technique as to the discolouration which has taken place over the course of centuries. Composed as it was with a high percentage of lead salts, white lead has become a beautiful black!

In contrast to this genre, the constant aim of court painters was to stylise the image based on reality, so as to produce a synthesis summarising the main features of the subject but without being a faithful copy. Whatever the form the court painter set out to represent, he laid down the outlines first, striving for harmony of line and following what is, in its way, an impressionistic view, an excellent way of emphasising the most significant aspect of the subject. According to Hsü Shên, the author of *Shuo wên chieh tzu,* the oldest known Chinese dictionary, 'painting *(hua)* consists of boundaries', a definition which shows the importance given to line and brush-stroke.

Paintings on silk or paper not of the popular or craftsman genre were presented in one of two ways: as a hand scroll (*makemono* in Japanese, i.e. something which is rolled up), or as a hanging scroll (*kakemono,* something which is hung up). Already common in the first centuries of the Christian era, the hand scroll derived from the illustrated book, by way of a gradual suppression of the written text which was eventually replaced by one long continuous composition. The hand scroll was intended to be read by unrolling one end and rolling up the other on the precious sticks which serve as 'souls' and as fastenings, so that it cannot be studied all at once. Like a book, it is to be enjoyed in detail as fast or as slow as one pleases. One may pause, now to study this point, now that, unwinding and winding up accordingly.

Made to be hung up and seen all at once, the *kakemono* appeared later than the *makemono,* during the T'ang dynasty (618-906 AD). It may have been suggested indirectly by wall tapestries or sacred pictures hung on walls. Neither the *kakemono* nor the *makemono* was meant for continual or prolonged exhibition. Mounted on precious silk with clasps of jade or ivory, each was wrapped in fine damask and shut away safely in a padded, scented box all to itself.

Naturally, the *makemono* offers an endless variety of views. To handle it expertly and discover them is quite a different pleasure from that given by the contemplation of framed pictures or wall paintings. Thus the size, shape and function of Chinese paintings have had an enormous influence on the development of perspective and composition, as have the fans and albums which appeared later on alongside the scrolls.

In the *kakemono,* which obviously favours tall compositions, recession is suggested not in the one continuous sweep of scientific perspective, but by a series of planes, one above the other. The most distant are at the top of the composition, and though their details receive less attention, they remain linked to the planes in the foreground by gentle gradation. But in the *makemono* the artist often accentuates the impression made by some detail to which he wants to draw the spectator's attention by correlating different elements.

As for subject-matter, Chinese painting can never be separated from the other aspects of the spiritual life, and all aesthetic criticism is concerned immediately with the religious and philosophical ideas of the various ages. For this reason, Chinese painting has had

13. Ku K'ai-chih (*c.* 344-*c.* 406). *The Nymph of the Lo River* (detail). Sung copy of the original scroll illustrating the poem of the same name by Ts'ao Chih. Freer Gallery of Art, Washington.

13. Ku K'ai-chih (*c. 344-c. 406*). *The Nymph of the Lo River* (detail). Sung copy of the original scroll illustrating the poem of the same name by Ts'ao Chih. Freer Gallery of Art, Washington. Even in the copy Ku K'ai-chih's stylistic characteristics stand out especially in the relationship between the trees and the human figures which the copyist, however, has made heavier.

14. Han Kan (active *c. 742-756*) (attributed). *Central Asiatic Grooms leading Horses offered in Tribute.* T'ang dynasty. Freer Gallery of Art, Washington. The characterisation of faces and costumes and the details of the horsecloths show a little known aspect of Han Kan's work. Hand-scroll on silk in colours and gold.

14

15. Chang Sêng-yu (beginning of the 6th century). *The Planet Saturn*. Municipal Museum, Osaka. Detail of the hand-scroll on silk in ink and colour called the *Five Planets and the Twenty-four Constellations.* Copy of the Sung dynasty which bears clear evidence of Indian inspiration in Saturn's anatomy and twisted dhoti.

16. Han Kan (active *c.* 742-756) (attributed). *Central Asiatic Groom with Two Horses*. T'ang dynasty. National Palace and Central Museum Collections, Taichung (Taiwan). Album leaf in ink and colour on silk. In this painting content is more important and the treatment more immediate than in the preceding work. This composition is accompanied by a good example of calligraphy.

15. Chang Sêng-yu (beginning of the 6th century). *The Planet Saturn*. Copy of the Sung dynasty. Municipal Museum, Osaka.

16. Han Kan (active *c.* 742-756) (attributed).
Central Asiatic Groom with Two Horses. T'ang dynasty.
National Palace and Central Museum Collections, Taichung
(Taiwan).

moral, ceremonial and even political importance. In his famous treatise, *Li tai ming hua chi* ('Record of Famous Paintings in Successive Ages', 845 AD), Chang Yen-yüan states that painting originated in nature, not in the works or will of man. Painting encourages culture and the principles of rectitude, he goes on to say. It was considered a creation of the gods, and in the beginning man used it to furnish examples of morality and 'mirrors of conduct'.

By and large, however, Chinese painters seldom give man a privileged place. Gradually, as the moral or educative interest diminishes or changes, more and more importance is assumed by nature, which tends to synthesise and arouse emotions often inexpressible in words, and in which man finds symbolic values and, above all, a universal harmony. A tiny human figure lost in a vast landscape is a detail of secondary if not negligible importance. If it has any meaning at all, it shows how nature rules over everything and succeeds in overwhelming man's tiny existence, while the relative proportions of man, trees and mountains are not only a symbol of man's inferiority but a reflection of the vastness of Chinese horizons as well. Yet, if the boundless plains, the rugged mountains, the gigantic rivers fill the mind with a sense of the infinite, uncontrollable power against which it is useless to struggle, the Chinese artist does not limit himself to discovering the vastness of the world around him. He knows that it arouses in his own mind, and in that of every sensitive cultured person, feelings of joy or sadness, terror or serenity, and he discovers that even a tiny hint can suffice to recall and revive a particular mood aroused by nature itself. A branch is enough, or a flower, or a bird on a tree, because over and above their symbolic value such things are the manifestations of a spirit deeply in tune with nature. Hence the custom among painters and poets of evoking seasons, points of light, moments in time, meteors, all by means of a simple detail, one that would in fact be lost in a gigantic picture but is isolated by the artist because it epitomises the essence of the whole scene.

In Chinese painting the importance assumed by nature meant that artists were not interested in the human body and avoided the nude, so much so that in the whole of Chinese art the only exceptions are the little female statues used for medical diagnosis. By the same token even covertly erotic emotions are excluded, and in works that treat of the *ars amandi* the illustrations are rough and unexciting. For all its equilibrium, however, Chinese painting is not immune to sensuality. Artists, literati and men of culture have an innate taste for beautiful materials and for the pleasing sensations of touch, smell and sight. The mounting, preservation and care of the scrolls provide ample opportunities to indulge all this. Yet, although such things reveal a subtle, almost morbid sensibility, they are only secondary effects and have nothing to do with true artistic creation.

17. Yen Li-pên (600-673). *The Payers of Tribute*. T'ang dynasty. National Palace and Central Museum Collections, Taichung (Taiwan).

17.   Yen Li-pên (600-673). *The Payers of Tribute.* T'ang dynasty. National Palace and Central Museum Collections, Taichung (Taiwan). Hand scroll in ink and colour on silk. The Western, Arab, Iranian and Indian types are easily recognisable by the precise characterisation of face and costume.

18.   Chou Fang (active *c.* 780-810) (attributed). *Ladies playing Music in the Garden* (detail). T'ang dynasty. W. Rockhill Nelson Gallery, Kansas City. Hand scroll in ink and colour on paper. A most delicate composition in which both garden and human figures are equally expressive.

19.   Yen Li-pên (600-673). *Portraits of the Emperors* (detail). T'ang dynasty. Museum of Fine Arts, Boston. Hand scroll on silk, copy. For all its having been conceived as a commemorative work, the picture is a clever attempt at portraiture vibrating with humanity.

20.   Anonymous 11th-century follower of Li Chao-tao (perhaps after an 8th-century work). *Emperor Ming Huang travelling in Shu.* National Palace and Central Museum Collections, Taichung (Taiwan). Hanging scroll in ink and colour on paper. Being wider than it is high, this is an unusual composition.

18. Chou Fang (active *c.* 780-810) (attributed). *Ladies playing Music in the Garden* (detail). T'ang dynasty. W. Rockhill Nelson Gallery, Kansas City.

晋武帝司馬炎

19. Yen Li-pên (600-673). *Portraits of the Emperors* (detail). T'ang dynasty. Museum of Fine Arts, Boston.

20. Anonymous 11th-century follower of Li Chao-tao (perhaps after an 8th-century work). *Emperor Ming Huang travelling in Shu.* National Palace and Central Museum Collections, Taichung (Taiwan).

Literature on the subject of artistic creation made its appearance at an early date, and what Chinese critics and teachers had to say about painting bears comparison with the more developed writings of the West. All criticism was based on the celebrated Six Principles of painting, defined for the first time at the end of the 5th century AD by Hsieh Ho in his famous work, *Ku hua p'in lu* ('Ancient Chronicle of the Classification of Painters'). Unfortunately, since each principle is synthesised in only four characters, the first and most important one, which contains the essence of the whole art of Chinese painting, is hard to understand entirely, so that the numerous translations differ widely one from the other. In Chinese it reads *'Ch'i yün sheng tung: Ch'i,* spirit or vital spirit, i.e. breath; *yün,* agreement or resonance; *sheng,* life; *tung,* movement. A free interpretation quoted by many is that of the great Japanese critic, Okakura Kakuzo: 'The life of the spirit in the rhythm of things.' Whatever the exact rendering of this much discussed principle, the gist is that the painter must grasp the essence of life by means of a personal 'tuning-in' on his own spirit (or perhaps, on his vital spirit).

Despite the obscurity of the text, the importance of the relationship between the 'spirit of the artist' and the life of the subject is brought out in an ancient treatise attributed to the 10th-century painter, Ching Hao. Written in the form of a dialogue between a wise old hermit and a young painter, it states that the defects due to a lack of *ch'i yün* ('tuning-in' of the spirit?) render compositions bizarre and dead, however good a technician the painter may be. Moreover, it goes on, the painter can do nothing to repair his mistakes. But if the composition has *ch'i yün* and is, therefore, a work of art, simple defects of ability do not spoil it.

The second principle lays down use of the brush for the essential structure of the subject represented, and the third obliges the painter to portray the subject faithfully. The fourth stipulates fidelity to the subject in the matter of colouring. The fifth lays down rules for the composition as a whole and its various elements. The sixth and last deals with the transmission of experience of the past by making copies.

Principles two to six can be learnt, but the first must be inborn. It 'grows in the silence of the soul', wrote Kuo Jo-hsü, one of the greatest critics of the Sung dynasty, in his *T'u hua chien wên chih* ('Notes on what is seen and felt [in] painting'), written in 1047. The first principle can be acquired neither by practice nor by ability because 'pictures are created in the mind, and emitted and revealed by the tip of the brush. The illusion of the shape of things is produced in a mysterious manner capable of arousing emotion in men and awakening the greatness of their souls.'

According to Tung Ch'i-ch'ang, the famous critic of the Ming dynasty, the first principle 'cannot be expressed in words'. It seems to correspond to Tao, the indefinable universal principle which is the basis of

Taoism. Like Tao, the first principle of painting cannot be acquired by an act of the will no matter how tenacious or enlightened. It results from a profound and complete spiritual and physical harmony with nature.

The similarity between the two principles, due to the need for an inexpressible harmony with the external world and also to the ambiguity of the term which shows the impossibility of precise definition, has given rise to talk of a 'pictorial Tao', the essence of Chinese painting. Thus words become genuine symbols, under cover of which are born a spiritual attitude and a vigorous precise style, two perfectly identifiable and definable things. Chang Yen-yüan makes this clear. This is what he says about the method of Wu Tao-tzu, a famous painter of the T'ang dynasty whose work we see now only in stereotyped carved stone reproductions: 'He concentrated his spirit and harmonised it with the works of nature, representing them with the power of his brush. His ideas were already firmly established before he began to paint: the completed picture expressed them all.' Like man, adds Chang Yen-yüan, the artist becomes the slave of external circumstances if his ideas are confused. Only when meditation and execution are fused into one single reality, independently of all desire to create a work of art, will he succeed in creating something valid. Chang Yen-yüan considered Wu Tao-tzu greater than any painter of the past, and greater than

21. Hsü Tao-ning (first half of the 11th century) (attributed). *Fishing in a Snowy River.* Sung dynasty. National Palace and Central Museum Collections, Taichung (Taiwan).

22. Anonymous (10th century). *Deer in an Autumnal Wood.* Five Dynasties. National Palace and Central Museum Collections, Taichung (Taiwan).

洞天山堂

23. After Tung Yüan (active *c*. 1000). *Pavilions on the Mountains of the Immortals.* Five dynasties. National Palace and Central Museum Collections, Taichung (Taiwan).

21.   Hsü Tao-ning (first half of the 11th century) (attributed). *Fishing in a Snowy River.* Sung dynasty. National Palace and Central Museum Collections, Taichung (Taiwan). Hanging scroll in ink and colour on silk. A characteristic composition in which man and his activities are reduced to nothing by the overpowering force of nature symbolised by the vertical mountains and the wide river.

22.   Anonymous (10th century). *Deer in an Autumnal Wood.* Five dynasties. National Palace and Central Museum Collections, Taichung (Taiwan). Detail of a hanging scroll in ink and colour on silk. Painted with a very acute sense of reality which uses both artifice in composition and poetic elan, this is one of the most beautiful examples of a 'quadrupeds and plants' picture.

23.   After Tung Yüan (active *c.* 1000). *Pavilions on the Mountains of the Immortals.* Five dynasties. National Palace and Central Museum Collections, Taichung (Taiwan). Hanging scroll in ink and colour on silk. The composition suggests an unreal superhuman world by stressing the contorted structure of rocks and trees and using the effect of mist in layers.

24.   *Buddhist Patriarch and Tiger.* Probably a 13th-century copy after Shih K'o (10th century). National Museum, Tokyo. Detail of one of the two hanging scrolls representing Buddhist patriarchs in mental harmony. It symbolises the state of calmness, assurance and mastery over external powers that can be reached by the technique of Buddhist meditation. Shih K'o treats the people he paints with violence and mastery and, perhaps unconsciously, a touch of caricature. According to tradition, all great Ch'an painting and Japanese Zen painting derives from him.

24. *Buddhist Patriarch and Tiger.* Probably a 13th-century copy after Shih K'o (10th century). National Museum, Tokyo.

any contemporary. Although he observed that the artist painted 'with frenzy' in a state of alcoholic inebriation, he considered him a real turning-point in Chinese painting. He was right. Most of the painters who came after Wu Tao-tzu copied his work and his technique. In the words of Su Tung-p'o (1036-1101), poet, painter and art critic, 'Some men have Tao and know art, others have Tao but do not know art: images form in their minds but do not take shape at their hands.'

Writers on painting often stressed technical ability and linked it with that of the calligrapher. 'All who succeed in calligraphy also succeed in painting because they bend the wrist and move the brush without difficulty', said the 15th-century painter T'ang Yin, one of the 'Four Great Masters'. What writers insisted on most, however, were the 'powers' which decided the conception of forms and symbols. They devoted much more space to the creative act and inspiration than to iconography, technique or style. In its way, theirs was a psychological approach aimed at studying the different artists and finding out what aspects of pictorial creation they had in common. The findings were tabulated and expounded in principles and statements whose meaning often seems obscure. Nevertheless, they were undoubtedly understood and deeply appreciated.

Like the principles, the symbols too were firm, clear and of a universal application. Thus the character and spirit of a gentleman were represented by bamboos, because, just as the bamboo combines strength with pliability and can appear cold and severe, or gentle and adaptable, so too a gentleman knows how to bend before the wind of misfortune without diverging from his ideals. That bamboos should have become one of the favourite subjects of painters is understandable. 'Among the painters of this world,' says Su Tung-p'o, 'some know how to represent form, but only gentlemen and men of genius can grasp the profound essence of things.' When they look at the compositions of Yü-k'o, a poor official venerated by succeeding generations as the greatest painter of bamboos who ever lived, 'everything is in its proper place just as nature created it, and the mind is satisfied because the compositions express the spirit of a gentleman.' In fact, 'when Yü-k'o painted bamboos, he was conscious neither of himself nor of his humanity, but only of bamboos.' And therein lay his greatness according to Chinese thinking, for whatever the dynasty, trend or style the truly great artist had to succeed in submerging his own personality if he wished to infuse life into the work he was creating. And if it was a question of painting a religious picture, the Chinese artist no less than the Indian had first to raise his mind to God so that he could adore him and express his presence.

The earliest examples of Chinese painting are found on protohistoric terracotta vases and other objects, and their presence on them had not only a decorative purpose but a religious and symbolic one as well. With the frequent use of curved lines, especially segments of an ellipse, their rough but substantial brushstrokes, their predilection for particular combinations of colour, the archaic geometrical designs are evidence of a taste that was to flourish again and again in succeeding ages. Nevertheless these ancient painted vases are in a class apart. They had little to do with the main output of painting which began much later.

Not counting the inevitable texts, all that remains of its initial stages are a few fragments and some murals in provincial tombs. From the texts we learn that the earliest paintings were done to commemorate some particular person or to point a moral. In his impressions of the great murals which adorned the imperial palaces, Ts'ao Chih (192-232) says: 'When you contemplate the painting which represents the Three Kings or the Five Emperors, you cannot help looking at them with respect and veneration. But when you see the *San chi* represented [the *San chi* were the last depraved sovereigns of the earliest mythological and historical dynasties] you cannot help feeling depressed. And when you see the portraits of rebels and unnatural sons you cannot help gnashing your teeth.'

Thus painting served both as a historical and as a day-to-day record, fulfilling the task both of commemoration (with highly imaginative characterisa-

25

25. Hui-tsung (1082-1135) (attributed). *Mountain Landscape with Autumn Colours.* Sung dynasty. National Palace and Central Museum Collections, Taichung (Taiwan).

26. Chao Po-chü (1120-1182) (attributed, but perhaps a 12th-century copy of the original). *Palaces of Han.* Sung dynasty. National Palace and Central Museum Collections, Taichung (Taiwan).

27. Li Lung-mien (1040-1106) (attributed). *The Reign of the Immortals* (detail). Signed Li Kung-lin (pseudonym). Sung dynasty. Freer Gallery of Art, Washington.

25. Hui-tsung (1082-1135) (attributed). *Mountain Land-scape with Autumn Colours*. Sung dynasty. National Palace and Central Museum Collections, Taichung (Taiwan). Hanging scroll in ink and a little colour on silk. The painter is striving to combine picture and text closely and the latter becomes an integral part of the composition.

26. Chao Po-chü (1120-1182) (attributed, but perhaps a 12th-century copy of the original). *Palaces of Han*. Sung dynasty. National Palace and Central Museum Collections, Taichung (Taiwan). Album leaf in ink and colour on silk. Dominated by the fabric of the palace, the composition really represents the traditional feast, 'Double Seven', in honour of various mythological personages, in which the court participates.

27. Li Lung-mien (1040-1106) (attributed). *The Reign of the Immortals* (detail). Signed Li Kung-lin (pseudonym). Sung dynasty. Freer Gallery of Art, Washington. Hand scroll in ink on paper. The metaphysical evanescence of the temple is framed in a stylised landscape rendered unreal by twisted trees and towering mountains. The Immortals are standing on the clouds.

28. Li Han-chung (1120-1160) (attributed). *Quail*. Sung dynasty. Nezu Art Museum, Tokyo. Album leaf in ink and colour on silk. Here the bird's feathers become almost a decorative motif but without altering the completely realistic structure of the composition.

28. Li Han-chung (1120-1160) (attributed). *Quail.*
Sung dynasty. Nezu Art Museum, Tokyo.

tion) and of documentation with a moral purpose. With the exception of two fragments on silk from a tomb at Ch'ang-sha in Hunan (southern central China) dating from about the 3rd century BC, all the other remains date from after the beginning of the Christian era. The fragments from Ch'ang-sha show that technically painting was already fully developed. The figures on the lacquered box preserved at Pyongyang in Korea give us an idea of the expressive characterisation used by painters at the end of the 1st century AD in their historical and didactic compositions. In both style and composition the murals from a tomb at Liao-yang in Manchuria are better paintings. One of them shows a procession of dignitaries in carriages with high wheels accompanied by horsemen whose mounts are at the 'flying gallop'. Standing out against the neutral background, the figures follow each other in graceful rhythm, a fine example of 'rhythmic perspective' in which scenic details are left to the imagination. The marked stylisation of both men and horses reveals an already refined taste. More complex, the second picture represents an entertainment with musicians, on the right, accompanying acrobats, jugglers and conjurors gathered round a big fountain which serves both for illusionistic effects and as scenery. Much superior both in style and quality are the terracotta tiles from a tomb in Honan (northern China) now in the Boston Museum of Fine Arts. The subject seems to be the celebration of the empresses' virtues. With the variety of attitudes and faces, the refined colouring and composition, the workmanship shows that under the later Han (1st-3rd centuries AD) Chinese artists were already masters of their tools.

The growing development of calligraphy was reflected in the varying intensity of outline, leading clearly to the exceptional virtuosity of later artists who abandoned anonymity and came out as definite personalities, individual masters with an individual style. The first name we have, and also one of the greatest, is Ku K'ai-chih (c. 344-c. 406). Ku K'ai-chih worked in Nanking, capital of the south, and had no contact with the semi-foreign culture of the north which was then dominated by the Wei dynasties of Turkish origin. Although a Taoist, he did not despise Confucianism, and painted Buddhist subjects when they pleased him. His spirit, his painting and the bewildering character of some of his compositions made the chronicles define him as a genius in many spheres. Bizarre, sensitive, his output was enormous but all that remains are copies of uneven merit and by different hands.

In this context the word 'copy' does not imply falsification. Like the ancient Romans the Chinese regarded copying as a means of diffusing works of art and making them available for study according to the last of the Six Principles. In any case even from copies one can get a good idea of Ku K'ai-chih's style—his love of slender lines, light colour, movements in the clothes of his figures, his deep interest in female figures, his original way of composing a picture which was not to find many later imitators. The most famous of all his works is *Admonitions of the Instructress to the Court Ladies*. The copy in the British Museum is probably a work of the T'ang dynasty, whereas *The Nymph of the Lo River* in the Freer Gallery, Washington, and *Landscape* in the Metropolitan Museum, New York, are undoubtedly much later copies, perhaps of the 12th century.

Chang Sêng-yu who flourished between 500 and 520 under the Liang dynasty, also worked in Nanking, but, unlike Ku K'ai-chih, he used chiaroscuro and preferred Buddhist subjects. His contemporaries regarded him as the greatest painter of the age. Whereas Ku K'ai-chih dominated the spirit of his creations, they said, Chang Sêng-yu was an absolute master of the anatomy and of 'the flesh' of the figures that he painted. This can be seen in the 11th- or 12th-century copy of *The Five Planets and Twenty-four Constellations*. Here the personification of Saturn on the bull which symbolises him looks like an Indian ascetic albeit seen through Chinese eyes. Moreover he is sitting in the position prescribed by Yoga for meditation. The anatomy and chiaroscuro, considering the period, show exceptional power of realism, and the picture as a whole is proof that China ignored neither iconographic hints nor technical tricks from foreign sources if they could be useful.

Recently united under the T'ang, China resumed her conquests and westward expansion. At this time poetry and painting reached very high levels. Of the great T'ang painting, however, little remains. The anti-Buddhist persecutions and the complex vicissitudes of the period brought about the destruction of large quantities of art treasures. Because access to the caves that contained them was difficult, the murals at Tun-huang on the central Asian border have been preserved. Inspired by the paradises and miraculous tales of Buddhism, the paintings are of great ascetic value, but the cosmopolitan culture which they reflect, a culture still redolent of Greece and Rome, makes them undoubtedly more central Asian than traditional Chinese. Together with another work undoubtedly by Chinese painters, the Horyuji murals at Nara in Japan, unfortunately destroyed by fire in 1949, they were the chief relics of a splendid artistic heritage and most important from a historical point of view as well.

As for the great court art, the texts tells of an extraordinary flowering of famous masters, listed in, for example, the *T'ang ch'ao ming hua lu* ('Celebrated Painters of the T'ang Dynasty'), where the author has classified them in order of merit. But apart from one of Han Kan's works, heavily restored, it is chiefly through copies that we acquire our knowledge of styles and trends.

Owing to the imperialist and expansionist policy

29. Ma Fên (end of the 11th century). *The Hundred Wild Geese.* Sung dynasty. Academy of Arts, Honolulu.

30. Ma Yüan (*c.* 1190-1224). *A Walk on a Mountain Path in Spring.* Sung dynasty. National Palace and Central Museum Collections, Taichung (Taiwan).

29. Ma Fên (end of the 11th century). *The Hundred Wild Geese.* Sung dynasty. Academy of Arts, Honolulu. Detail of a hand-scroll in ink on silk. Note how the artist has caught the flight of geese—each bird in a different position, and the beating of their wings frozen in seemingly successive attitudes. Reminiscent of a slow-motion film, the composition shows Ma Fên's remarkable memory and power of observation, qualities which rank him among the cleverest and most devoted animal painters from prehistoric times to his own.

30. Ma Yüan (*c.* 1190-1224). *A Walk on a Mountain Path in Spring.* Sung dynasty. National Palace and Central Museum Collections, Taichung (Taiwan). Album leaf in ink and light colour on silk. Composition with that individual method of foreshortening which clearly shows why the author was nicknamed 'One-corner Ma'.

31. Ma Yüan (*c.* 1190-1224). *Lone Fisherman.* Sung dynasty. National Museum, Tokyo. Hand-scroll in ink on silk. One of the most beautiful and famous of all Chinese paintings. The solitude of the fisherman is a symbol of the isolation of man. Ma Yüan uses the raw surface of the silk to represent the wide ocean.

32. Anonymous. *Portrait of the Ch'an master Wu-chün.* Hanging scroll dated 1238. Sung dynasty. Temple Collection, Tofukuji, Kyoto. Hanging scroll in ink and very brilliant colour on silk, dated 1238. This is a fine example of a type of portraiture done for commemorative and religious purposes, if not actually for worship. That it differs from symbolic and interpretative portraiture is evident from the use of colour and the striving for resemblance.

31. Ma Yüan (*c.* 1190-1224). *Lone Fisherman.* Sung
dynasty. National Museum, Tokyo.

32. Anonymous. *Portrait of the Ch'an master Wu-chün.*
Hanging scroll dated 1238. Sung dynasty. Temple
Collection, Tofukuji, Kyoto.

followed by the emperors, T'ang painting had a strong political slant. In contrast, poetry reflected an entirely different, pre-eminently spiritual attitude and with some of the most effective compositions on the horrors of war ever written.

One popular subject for painters was horses, a reflection of foreign tradition and customs, and a choice suggested at home by the fact that the emperors used to rear them in thousands. The leading artist in this field was Han Kan (active between 742 and 756). So greatly was he interested that legends began to be told of his magical capacity to make his horses 'live', although the critics would have it that he paid more attention to the flesh than to the bone structure. Of the humblest origin, Han Kan trained under the great Wang Wei, an occasional customer at the inn where Han Kan was a waiter. Later Han Kan won the admiration and protection of the Emperor Ming Huang. In the list of famous T'ang painters he is classified among those 'gifted with inspiration', which meant that, although among the great, he was in the lowest group of this class.

Better than Han Kan but not as good as Wu Tao-tzu was Chou Fang, a most sensitive interpreter of court life, especially as it concerned the imperial ladies. With him there began some attempt at psychological enquiry, limited, however, to isolated moods with no idea of their cause or effect.

During the T'ang dynasty, both court painters and

muralists took ever increasing interest in landscape. A good example of work in this specialist field is *The Emperor Ming Huang travelling in Shu* (Plate 20). The picture illustrates that desperate flight in 756 from the rebellious capital to a far-off city. Coming out of a gorge and crossing over bridges through a glade, the royal party starts to ascend a rugged mountain overhanging immense valleys. Although the countryside is in flower, a sense of danger exudes from the great neatly split rocks that threaten the path which the horsemen must take. The scroll has been preserved for us by an anonymous copyist of the 11th century. Judging by the style, the original may well be the work of Li Ssu-hsün (*c.* 651-*c.* 715/19) or of his son Li Chao-tao (*c.* 675-*c.* 730). Both were outstanding landscapists and founded the northern school. But, on the other hand, there is nothing of the Li style in the sense of growing discomfort to the travellers suggested by the landscape itself as they advance towards the overhanging rocks lit with a pinkish light that seems to come from below. In accordance with the contemporary style, there are no shadows, yet their absence in no way diminishes the effect of light.

To complete this glimpse of T'ang painting, a period in which lived so many artists of whom nothing is now left except their names and brief critical notices, three should be mentioned: Yen Li-pên (active 627-650), keen observer of foreign manners and customs and, as can be seen from a famous scroll,

Portraits of the Emperors, now in the Boston Museum of Fine Arts, a painter particularly interested in commemorative themes; Wei-ch'ih I-seng, a foreigner from central Asia and a specialist in Buddhist themes and pictures of monsters or of fantasies; and Wang Wei to whom is attributed a portrait of the Confucian philosopher Fu Sheng.

After the T'ang came what are called the Five Dynasties. For painting it was both a period of great output and a prelude to the glorious Sung dynasty. The painting of the Five Dynasties, varied and highly original, echoed the political division of the country which took place at this time. Moreover it seems to have acquired greater freedom thereby. Yet, though 'non-conformist' tendencies predominated in the north, and 'decadent' ones in the south, there were no strong local trends that could have been defined geographically.

This was the period which saw the birth of the monochrome landscape, painted as though the artist had succeeded in penetrating a real landscape and in reproducing its essence as did the first painters to be inspired by Ch'an, the meditative form of Buddhism, recently introduced into China. (In Japan, where it was known as Zen, this system of philosophy was to have still greater success.) Of supreme importance but loaded with symbolism, Ch'an painting influenced the technique of ink-painting and diverted interest from painting in colours during the T'ang dynasty.

The picture of the Buddhist patriarch and the tiger (Plate 24), considered an original work of Shih K'o, though it is more probably a much restored copy of the Sung dynasty, gives an idea of the impetuous immediacy of Ch'an painting and its connection with calligraphy (the strongest strokes imitate the so-called 'grass' writing).

Another innovation during the Five Dynasties were the motifs of 'flowers and birds' and of 'quadrupeds and plants'. The success of these motifs indirectly reflects the Chinese spirit of concentration, which was increased by the practice of Ch'an, by which a Chinese could 'see a world in a grain of sand, and a Heaven in a wild flower'. But the most successful of all was the 'mountains and water' motif—in other words, landscape. It became the favourite theme of Chinese artists, and in it they found the means for expressing not only their romantic sensibility but the depths of their souls as well.

A list of the subjects painted by Chinese artists during the Sung dynasty and the Mongol period is given in the preface to the large catalogue, dated 1120, of the emperor Hui-tsung's collection. First come Taoist and Buddhist subjects, then human affairs, followed by palaces and other buildings, foreign peoples, dragons and fish, landscapes, animals, flowers and birds, bamboos in ink, and lastly vegetables and fruit. The list thus covers religion, psychology, ethnology and architecture. The attention paid to 'bamboos in

33. Ma Lin (active *c.* 1220). *Awaiting Friends by Lantern-Light.* Sung dynasty. National Palace and Central Museum Collections, Taichung (Taiwan).

34. Li Sung (1166-1243). *Hangchow Bay by Moonlight.*
Sung dynasty. National Palace and Central Museum
Collections, Taichung (Taiwan).

35. Hsai Kuei (*c.* 1180-1230). *Talking with a Friend under Pines by a Precipice.* National Palace and Central Museum Collections, Taichung (Taiwan).

33. Ma Lin (active *c.* 1220). *Awaiting Friends by Lantern-Light.* Sung dynasty. National Palace and Central Museum Collections, Taichung (Taiwan). Album leaf in ink and colour on silk, inspired by a poem by Li Po. With the distances compressed, this is a study of twilight which brings out the dark mass of the house, the illuminated interior and the white figure of the waiting host.

34. Li Sung (1166-1243). *Hangchow Bay by Moonlight.* Sung dynasty. National Palace and Central Museum Collections, Taichung (Taiwan). Album leaf in ink and colour on paper. By the light of the moon, the opaqueness of the slender buildings contrasts with the half-light of the ocean furrowed with a stylised wave of surf.

35. Hsai Kuei (*c.* 1180-1230). *Talking with a Friend under Pines by a Precipice.* National Palace and Central Museum Collections, Taichung (Taiwan). Hand scroll in ink on silk. The environment and the landscape act upon the two friends who seem to be absorbed by it.

36. Liang K'ai (active at the beginning of the 13th century). *The Poet Li Po.* Property of the Cultural Properties Protection Commission, Tokyo. Hanging scroll in ink on paper. This famous imaginary portrait is perhaps the artist's masterpiece.

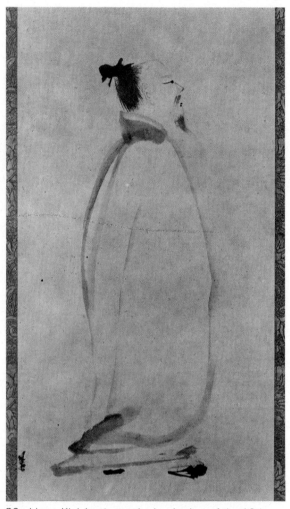

36. Liang K'ai (active at the beginning of the 13th century). *The Poet Li Po*. Property of the Cultural Properties Protection Commission, Tokyo.

ink' is shown by the fact that this subject is a category all on its own, while the importance of landscapes is similarly stressed, as are also the 'flowers and birds' motif and the two groups 'animals' and 'vegetables', sometimes united, as we have already seen, in the special form of composition 'quadrupeds and plants'. In some ways the list seems to give unusual importance to man, his mind and his affairs, but if one studies the psychological values which the Chinese artists sought under these ten headings, especially under those which do not refer to man, one will see that they are things almost completely unknown in the West although the West can understand them once it discovers their hidden meanings. For the Chinese artist, plants and animals are not mere physical presences, nor are landscapes just representations of places. All have a direct connection with something infinitely vast and, one might say, indefinable, as the very life of nature itself, for which Chinese artists feel an almost mystical propensity. This is what makes them seek effects of light in the changing seasons, in the passage of time, in different atmospheric conditions. The Chinese artist's strength lies in his ability to study nature in its various guises, and then to gather from it and express that which is capable of communicating a given mood to a sensitive spectator. At the same time he synthesises what he sees and eliminates anything superfluous or not strictly necessary to his purpose.

Thus even before the Sung period there came into vogue a tormented, almost primordial landscape with fantastic mountain peaks, rocks like 'the bones of the earth', fissures, cliffs, above all with exhaustive attempts at rendering the erosion and stratification of the rocks, which have now taken on a symbolic and poetic significance, while the rushing water, in streams and cascades, is made to represent the goodness, the charity, the very life of the earth animating the inert weight of the massive mountains. In painting them the artist seems to have observed the landscape from a faraway high vantage point whence details and colours merge into an almost unreal projection on the far horizon, lost at times in the infinite void of the neutral background. Astonished Westerners have seen in Sung and Yüan landscapes the unknown forerunners of Impressionism. But in reality the relationship can be seen, on closer examination, to be more a case of wishful thinking than a well based fact, and modern critics have accused Sung and Yüan painters of excessive sweetness, taken them to task for their 'sickly' sentimentality and the complete absence of sensitivity towards problems of contemporary society.

For a number of reasons, not excluding those arising from favourable references to Chinese critical works of the Ming and Ch'ing periods (especially the second), people have been led to praise the painting of those times which, in part at least, is less sweet even if, on many grounds, it remains equally out of touch with those problems which seem to us of more immediate significance. Historically, however, notwithstanding the success of the Imperial Academy, the Sung period is undoubtedly the most intensively creative of all in the evolution of Chinese painting; it is the richest in problems, the richest in promise. 'Being convinced of the unity of the universe,' a modern Chinese critic writes, 'the Chinese artist (and the Far East in general) refuses to halt reality in a single instant of time or to localise it in a definite point in space.' The same universal tendencies of today should lead to a reassessment of the Sung and Yüan periods, an age when this attitude was particularly strong, unless the undisputed and irrepressible pictorialism of Chinese artists be a barrier to an objective critical reappraisal.

The Sung dynasty was founded, as a sequel to a military revolt, by Chao K'uang-yin, a most able general who was acclaimed emperor by the armed forces of all China. Historically the dynasty saw the start of a period of peace which lasted nearly a hundred years although Peking was partly occupied all that time by the Khitans, a barbaric people of pre-Mongol origin. In the face of many difficulties the Confucian literati carried out many wise political changes, and these, especially the agrarian reforms, led to a complete reassessment of the whole of Chinese culture. With the emperor Hui-tsung (1101-1125), a painter and a highly cultured and sensitive man (he was called the 'dreamer with a crown'), the Sung dynasty

37. Anonymous (late 11th century). *Literary Nobleman under a Willow*. Sung dynasty. National Palace and Central Museum Collections, Taichung (Taiwan).
38. Ma Lin (active *c.* 1220). *Listening to the Wind among the Pines*. Sung dynasty. National Palace and Central Museum Collections, Taichung (Taiwan).

reached its highest point—and also its lowest, thanks to the alliance with the Jurchen, semi-savage nomads from Manchuria. Suddenly turning violently hostile, they conquered the capital and captured Hui-tsung and his elder son. Northern China fell into the hands of the barbarians but the Sung dynasty lived on in the south under the guidance of Hui-tsung's younger son.

Although China was thus politically divided, there is no doubt that later Chinese art critics were unwise to divide Sung painting into north and south. Their object was to establish a yardstick: paintings of the south were to be accepted, those from the north rejected. Although in practice there were no differences in trends or styles that could be geographically local-

39. Mu-ch'i (*c.* 1210-1275). *Scenes of the Hsiao and Hsiang Rivers* (detail). Sung dynasty. Nezu Art Museum, Tokyo.

ised, this arbitrary distinction has given rise to much confusion and misunderstanding. As far as we are concerned, therefore, the term 'Northern Sung' refers exclusively to the period preceding the imprisonment and death of Hui-tsung, and 'Southern Sung' to the following period.

Another cause of confusion was the existence of an academy in the south of the Sung territory. Chinese critics of the Ming period and to a lesser degree Western critics of the 1950s, attacked the work of the Sung painters who gravitated to this centre for ideological reasons which, as often happens, had nothing to do with the artistic merit or the creative ability of those artists.

37.   Anonymous (c. end of the 11th century). *Literary Noble-man under a Willow.* Sung dynasty. National Palace and Central Museum Collections, Taichung (Taiwan). Hanging scroll in ink and colour on silk. It shows T'ao Yüan-ming, a 4th-century poet, who retired from the court to live in the country where he became a symbol of solitude. Concentration and creative power are indicated by the white scroll and the wine in the wide cup. The willow alludes with delicacy to the sensual grace of the poet's thoughts.

38.   Ma Lin (active c. 1220). *Listening to the Wind among the Pines.* Sung dynasty. National Palace and Central Museum Collections, Taichung (Taiwan). Hanging scroll in ink and colour on silk, with seal dated 1246. One of the best of those paintings which bring the refined sensibility of a cultured man in direct contact with nature and its harmony.

39.   Mu-ch'i (c. 1210-1275). *Scenes of the Hsiao and Hsiang Rivers* (detail). Sung dynasty. Nezu Art Museum, Tokyo. Detail of a hand-scroll in ink on paper. The protagonist of the picture is the dying evening light which, together with the mist, en-velops the river and the mountains and seems to reduce to nothing the affairs of man.

40.   Mi Fu (1051-1107) (attributed). *Pines and Mountains in Spring.* Sung dynasty. National Palace and Central Museum Collections, Taichung (Taiwan). Hanging scroll in ink and colour on silk. Mi Fu's ability as a painter shows itself in the great mass of mountains, in the stylisation of the pines, in the slowly lifting mist in a landscape which has become abstract in the painter's mind.

40. Mi Fu (1051-1107) (attributed). *Pines and Mountains in Spring.* Sung dynasty. National Palace and Central Museum Collections, Taichung (Taiwan).

Critics and literati of the Ming and Ch'ing dynasties considered it morally wrong to be a professional artist: the Wên-jên hua, or literati style, decreed that the art of painting and that of calligraphy should be ends in themselves. But this did not prevent the Sung phase becoming the most sensitive turning point in the output of Chinese painting. In fact it gave rise to the literati painting of which future generations were to be so proud. Apart from Hui-tsung who was excessively praised or excessively criticised on account of his political position and his ideological attitude to aesthetics, the array of Sung painters undoubtedly includes a remarkable group of very great men. Hui-tsung himself, who both as a painter and collector preferred the birds and flowers motif, was an artist of outstanding intelligence, a formidable expert and undoubtedly the most cultured and sensitive of all the Chinese emperors. He tried landscapes too, and if we had a complete list of his works we should have a much clearer idea of the changes of taste in his reign. For the rest we know from the chronicles of his day that he used to urge his artists in the academy to practise a profound realism which should in certain ways be extremely detailed.

The academy obeyed his orders promptly. The fact that it did not have a deadening effect and become an obstacle to the free flowering of artistic creation is shown by the quality of the works which it produced and the variation of its styles. This seems to indicate that Hui-tsung's control was most enlightened and effective, quite different from what might have happened if his precepts had been followed too slavishly.

The painting of the Sung period as a whole differed according to the subjects represented. Works of a sacred or documentary character had no need to search for a style as had secular painting, nor did it make use of the synthesising expressionism of the Ch'an Buddhist style. The portrait of the Ch'an master, Wu-chun, an anonymous work dated 1238, is enough to show the importance of the realistic portrait, free from all metaphysical and symbolic significance and particularly suitable as just a cult object. Similarly a Sung painter, Chao Po-chü (1120-1182), specialised in landscapes where the works of man predominated, thus almost reversing the traditional role of nature. For him nature had poetic value only when it bore the evident stamp of man's domination. The painting on the page of an album entitled *Palaces of Han* is certainly a work of the end of the 12th or the beginning of the 13th century, but the title is misleading. In reality, the artist is concerned not so much with the palace, illuminated inside, as with the preparations afoot for a traditional festival, 'Double Seven', which terminates with contemplation of the moon, emphasising the participation of the empress and her suite. According to tradition the picture is by Chao Po-chü, yet, although repeatedly made, the attribution is wrong. But one can see that the anonymous painter was following the style and spirit of Chao Po-chü, and this in itself is proof of the existence of a pictorial style completely divorced from the traditional Chinese interpretation of nature.

As a painter of historical or legendary episodes, Li Han-chung stands alongside Chao Po-chü. He lived from about 1120 to 1160, and painted a famous picture showing the Lady Ts'ai-yen returning home to China after a twelve-year exile among the barbarians (the Hsiung-nu who later, under the name of the Huns, invaded Europe). But Li Han-chung painted animals too, and of course landscape. From Ma Fên, active towards the end of the 11th century and famous for his scroll *The Hundred Wild Geese,* there derived a whole dynasty of painters of whom the most remarkable were Ma Fên's grandson, the landscape artist Ma Yüan (active *c.* 1190-1224), and Ma Yüan's son, Ma Lin (active *c.* 1220-1250). Together with Hsia Kuei (*c.* 1180-1230), they are the greatest landscape artists of the academy of the Southern Sung. Ma Yüan invented a new way of rendering perspective which made use of the delicate evanescence of colour tones, and won him the nickname 'One-corner Ma' because he put the foreground figures in one corner of the composition, and then, by means of a diagonal passage of figures or objects getting fainter and fainter, separated the foreground figures from the opposite corner which he left empty or, better, open to the infinite. The picture thus created was impressive because it

41. Sun Chün-tse (*c.* 1300). *Landscape*. Yüan
dynasty. Seikado Foundation, Tokyo.

42. Chao Mêng-fu (1254-1322) (attributed). Copy, for study purposes, of Wang Wei's *Wang-Ch'uan*. Yüan dynasty. British Museum, London.

41. Sun Chün-tse (*c.* 1300). *Landscape.* Yüan dynasty. Seikado Foundation, Tokyo. Hanging scroll in ink and colour on silk. The pavilion among the pines, the waterfall and the background of overhanging mountains which form the gorge are interpreted in a calm manner which, although hinting at the power of nature, has nothing wild or awesome about it.

42. Chao Mêng-fu (1254-1322) (attributed). Copy, for study purposes, of Wang Wei's *Wang-Ch'uan.* Yüan dynasty. British Museum, London. Hand scroll in ink and colour on silk. Notice the striving for style in a landscape of water and mountains.

43. Chao Mêng-fu (1254-1322). *Autumn Colours on the Chao and Hua Mountains* (detail). Hand scroll dated 1295. Yüan dynasty. National Palace and Central Museum Collections, Taichung (Taiwan). Hand scroll in ink and colour on paper. The layout of the landscape is well matched by the half-tone colours, especially the greyish-blue of the distant mountains which become creations of the imagination.

44. Wang Mêng (1308-1385). *Hut in the Autumn Hills.* Yüan dynasty. National Palace and Central Museum Collections, Taichung (Taiwan). Hanging scroll in ink and colour on silk. The restlessly undulating lines of the hills contrast with the man-made orderliness of the buildings.

43. Chao Mêng-fu (1254-1322). *Autumn Colours on the Chao and Hua Mountains* (detail). Hand scroll dated 1295. Yüan dynasty. National Palace and Central Museum Collections, Taichung (Taiwan).

44. Wang Mêng (1308-1385). *Hut in the Autumn Hills.* Yüan dynasty. National Palace and Central Museum Collections, Taichung (Taiwan).

43

44

sharply contrasted the symbolic immaterial void of the infinite and the bold clear lines of the figures. In the same way Hsia Kuei often simplified and lightened the inert masses in his compositions, as in his *Talking with a Friend under Pines by a Precipice*. But in his great scroll *Ten Thousand Li of the Long River* the rocks and the earth are treated with 'speckled' brush-strokes, a partially impressionistic touch which is totally different and which was to be followed, though less strikingly, by other painters. Ma Yüan was rightly considered one of the greatest painters of all time, but Hsia Kuei, whose strong contrasts of black and white led one critic to refer to his 'virile brushwork' was not much inferior, even in the opinion of his contemporaries. On the other hand, Ma Lin was fond of the effects of light. In his *Awaiting Friends by Lantern-light* (Plate 33), the sharp relief assumed by the house in the clear evening light harmonises with the illuminated figure of the gentleman in white waiting in the hall. Of a different type and belonging to a special sort of subject is his scroll *Listening to the Wind among the Pines*, signed, sealed and dated 1246. This is the type of picture in which the principal subject is a literary man giving himself up to profound meditation suggested by some particular contemplative feeling. The real protagonist of such paintings, which occasionally have a sort of counterpart in poetry, is the feeling of the natural setting re-created in precise, minute but restricted indications of landscape. Paintings of this sort are, it should be said, the result of being able to use all the means provided by a fully developed art to express, graphically and from the outside, feelings and fantasies which should really be almost entirely excluded from painting, for they can only be made clear with the help of symbols and facial expressions. In Ma Lin's *Listening to the Wind among the Pines* the face of the larger of the two men shows that, although the branches and the pine-needles are still, he can hear the rustling of the pines. In a scroll by an anonymous 11th-century painter, *Literary Nobleman under a Willow* (Plate 37), the man's concentration is conveyed by the fixity of his gaze, while the wine cup and the paper show that he is seeking literary inspiration. Both paintings are of a high quality, but the genius with which Ma Lin renders the thoughts suggested by the wind makes his superior.

Small wonder that, with such sensitivity as this, Sung artists drew their animals and plants with the colour, compositional and descriptive effects with which we have recently been made familiar, as James Cahill remarks, by photography. But Chinese compositions are very much richer in those human vibrations which only creative power enlightened by genius is capable of giving us. And this creative power, this arrogant genius, is nowhere so evident as in the works inspired by Ch'an thought.

Liang K'ai, who became a Ch'an Buddhist priest, used a 'minimising brush-stroke', thus breaking every tie with tradition. Active from about 1200, he showed his power of expression in the exceptional sensitivity of his lines, in the reduction of the drawing to a bare minimum, and in his indisputable ability to obtain his brush effects on silk which are all the more marvellous because once the brush-stroke was made it could not be corrected. Generally accepted as one of the finest Chinese paintings, his imaginary portrait of Li T'ai-po, the great T'ang poet, is a famous example of his work. But before him the ranks of Sung painters had already been enriched with some resounding names. There had been, for example, Mi Fei (1051-1107), perhaps a foreigner, who was a man of wide culture as well as a painter and calligrapher. He had a strong bent for impressionistic observation and invented a particular sort of perspective which the Chinese in admiration called *mi yüan* ('lost distance') and which we might name 'atmospheric perspective'. The importance of Mi Fei in the field of criticism and in the evolution of Chinese painting style and theory which followed cannot be exaggerated.

Another well known name is Li Lung-mien (*c.* 1045-1106). Although from a family of literati (i.e. Confucianist), he also painted Buddhist subjects, landscapes and horses. Of works that have been handed down to us, we have his wonderful Khotan stallion accompanied by his groom which has become famous. Mu-ch'i (*c.* 1210-*c.* 1275) had the good fortune to be appreciated during his lifetime not only in China but in Japan as well. Sometimes violent, sometimes full of sweet sadness, his work has something of the work of Liang K'ai at times, and these two are undoubtedly the greatest Ch'an painters of the age. In Mu-ch'i's landscapes can be seen the virtuosity acquired by followers of the 'unconventional' Ch'an manner, and from him derive some aspects of Japanese Zen painting. A particularly successful picture of his, which Western eyes can appreciate too, is a landscape which forms part of a hand scroll now in Tokio, *Scenes of the Hsiao and Hsiang Rivers*. This scene is a free interpretation of a moment at twilight. Contrast this with a completely different picture, Mu-ch'i's amazing *Sparrows on a Branch,* a symbolic yet poetic composition where the two birds represent the rhythm of life and the power of nature.

The Mongol storm which burst over China had a remarkable result in the field not only of politics but also of art. We can divide the painters known to us into three groups. To the first belong those who strove to carry on the Sung tradition. Besides Ch'ien Hsüan (1235-1290), a good but not great painter, there was the landscape artist Sun Chün-tzu whose style and power of expression earned him a place all to himself.

The second group avoided archaising tendencies stemming from a desire to keep Sung painting alive, and set out to revive the styles of the more remote past and adapt them to the new age. The most repre-

45. Ni Tsan (1301-1374). *Landscape.* Hand scroll dated
1362. Yüan dynasty. Freer Gallery of Art, Washington.

46. Ni Tsan (1301-1374). *Landscape*. Yüan
dynasty. National Museum, Stockholm.

45. Ni Tsan (1301-1374). *Landscape.* Yüan dynasty. Freer Gallery of Art, Washington. Hand scroll in ink on paper dated 1362. The landscape is rendered with calm, meditated brush-strokes in the layout and style which Ni Tsan always used and which never lost their freshness.

46. Ni Tsan (1301-1374). *Landscape*. Yüan dynasty. National Museum, Stockholm. Hanging scroll in ink on paper. Here the brush seems to follow the erosion of the rocks and the shadows reflected in the water with delicacy and precision.

47. Shêng Mou (active *c.* 1310-1361). *On the River in Autumn.* Hand scroll in ink and colour on paper, with text by a friend of the painter, dated 1361. Yüan dynasty. National Palace and Central Museum Collections, Taichung (Taiwan). Apart from the originality of the scene, the chief characteristic of this painting is its softness and variety of colour.

48. Wu Chên (1280-1354). *Rocks and Bamboo.* Yüan dynasty. British Museum, London. Album leaf in ink on silk. Although Chinese critics consider Wu Chên's works 'calm and relaxed', the agitated leaves and the stem of the bamboo bent by the wind are intended to symbolise the struggle against adversity.

天際浮嵐送千山
草木扶亦江嶺止

錫山馮唐書
傷相逢將美泊
輕雲摩漁艇無常
拍礦流水清帝滂

日明
何自哭

浦山首西山蒼
桂莖蘭漿近前
雨竹蕭蕭為他生
妙化江烟浪平

天台萬一鼎
了無蹤跡到人間
不情功名身貴
笑語舡頭飽有山

47. Shêng Mou (active *c.* 1310-1361). *On the River in Autumn*. Hand scroll, with text by a friend of the painter, dated 1361. Yüan dynasty. National Palace and Central Museum Collections, Taichung (Taiwan).

48. Wu Chên (1280-1354). *Rocks and Bamboo*. Yüan
dynasty. British Museum, London.

sentative of them all is Chao Mêng-fu (1254-1322) who, although a descendant of the Sung imperial family, accepted service with the Mongols. He was a calligrapher and landscapist, and also a painter of horses which he represented with dry precise realism. Unlike Han Kan and Li Lung-mien, those earlier great painters of horses who preferred showing isolated animals, Chao Mêng-fu always grouped his and showed them in complete liberty. He was soon considered one of the greatest Chinese painters. His *Autumn Colours on Ch'iao and Hua Mountains* (Plate 43) is a truly revolutionary work—anti-romantic, cold, almost sinister in its stylisation, the landscape has the force of a primitive creation oppressed by the massive gloomy blue mountain, a clumsy monster standing out against the horizon. Kao K'o-kung, a dilettante painter (1248-1310), attempted a synthesis of past styles like Chao Mêng-fu before him. But, for all the critics' praises—they talked of his mountains as 'creations of the spirit' or 'mountains born in the depths of the soul'—he achieved no real originality.

The third group consisted of the four great Yüan masters, and it was their activity, together with some minor artists, which characterised the second part of the Mongol period. Huang Kung-wang (1269-1354), Wu Chên (1280-1354), Ni Tsan (1301-1374) and Wang Mêng (1310-1385) have every right to be called great masters. They were successors of the ancient tradition and forerunners of that which followed.

Huang Kung-wang, the oldest of the four, tackled the problem of landscape by drawing from life, and his pictures were highly original. To him Chinese painting owes the terraced structure of mountains which was to be so successful in later periods. Like Ni Tsan, Wu Chên withdrew from the world towards the end of his life and dedicated himself to painting and poetry. He was a painter of bamboo and a fine landscape artist. If we are to believe the stories about his wife's jealousy of his richer colleague, he was a rival of Shêng Mou (active *c.* 1310-1361) but infinitely superior to him in his profound interpretation of nature and in the detachment with which he painted, carefully excluding genre scenes from his work. The momentary success of Shêng Mou was due to the quality of his colours and his realistic details which, however, like that of the two men talking in the adjoining boats in his *On the River in Autumn* (Plate 47) are no more than whimsicalities.

The greatest, or at least the most brilliant, of the four and the one about whom we have precise biographical details is Ni Tsan. His use of a very dry brush was ideally suited to his artistic personality. He created marvellous pictures with a realistic fore-shortening of the landscape, which, because of his technique, could only be done on paper. Unlike Wu Chên, when the Mongol regime began to show signs of ending, he disposed of all his goods, great art collection and all, and wandered round China. From the poems, models of calligraphy, which accompany his pictures it is impossible to guess the hardship which his aimless wandering must have entailed. He transformed this self-imposed pilgrimage into a series of idyllic journeys and produced marvellous pictures and poems full of quotations from Taoism and Buddhism.

Shortly after Ni Tsan came Wang Mêng who, in his pictures, especially those in the 'literati style' revived the fantastic power of the first landscapists. He trained as a painter under his uncle, Chao Mêng-fu. At times the torments which beset his life seemed to be reflected in his work, in that nightmare of rugged landscapes with their pitted rocks. He died a political prisoner in a Ming dungeon. And yet it was through him that the experience of the Yüan period was directly transmitted to the first painters of the Ming period.

The Mongol dominion came to an end as the direct result of a most serious economic crisis that shook the southern regions. Revolts of great violence took place one after the other, directed not only against the Mongols but against the wealthy landowners and foreign merchants too. The driving force was a secret society called the 'White Lotus'. It organised the peasants and sought both social change and a return to ancient Chinese traditions. The leader was an able ex-Buddhist monk, Chu Yüan-chang, son of a miserably poor peasant. Having overcome his

49. Tai Chin (active at the beginning of the 15th century).
Returning Home at Evening in Spring. Ming dynasty.
National Palace and Central Museum Collections, Taichung
(Taiwan)

50. Shên Chou (1427-1509). *Two Fishermen on the River of the Plane Trees*. Ming dynasty. Academy of Arts, Honolulu.

49.   Tai Chin (active at the beginning of the 15th century). *Returning Home at Evening in Spring.* Ming dynasty. National Palace and Central Museum Collections, Taichung (Taiwan). Hanging scroll in ink and light colour on paper. In this landscape, lit by the last light of day, the moment of homecoming becomes a poetic motif.

50.   Shên Chou (1427-1509). *Two Fishermen on the River of the Plane Trees.* Ming dynasty. Academy of Arts, Honolulu. Hanging scroll in ink and colour on paper. Executed in a dry and clear style, with its fanciful perspective, this work illustrates a poem dated 1477, but both painting and poem are at least six years earlier.

51.   Wên Chêng-ming (1470-1559). *Pines and Cypresses by the Waterfall.* Ming dynasty. National Palace and Central Museum Collections, Taichung (Taiwan). Hanging scroll in ink and colour on silk dated 1584. In this work the 77 year old Wên Chêng-ming gives the full measure of his skill as a painter and all his experience as a calligrapher. The interwoven branches in a space without depth become an abstract motif reinforced by the white strip of the waterfall.

52.   Wên Chêng-ming (1470-1559). *The Farewell.* Ming dynasty. Vannotti Collection, Lugano. Hanging scroll in ink and a slight colour-wash on paper, signed and dated 1531. Even to a casual observer the sense of complete detachment is very clearly rendered by the relationship of the men to the trees, twisted and indifferent.

51

52. Wên Chêng-ming (1470-1559). *The Farewell.*
Hanging scroll signed and dated 1531. Ming
dynasty. Vannotti Collection, Lugano.

nearest rival, Ch'en Yu-liang, son of a fisherman, he conquered the lands which Ch'en had occupied (Honan, Hopei, Kiangsi), took Peking (1368) and became master of all China. All this happened within the space of three years, but before the end of that time he had already proclaimed himself Emperor. Showing as it did that he intended to follow tradition again, this calmed the apprehensions of the magistrates, the officials and the literati, all long since wearied of the Mongol regime. A great bloodbath put an end to the Yüan dynasty, the 'Great Beginning' (Ta-Yüan) as it had been called by the descendants of Genghis Khan. And with that bloodbath began 'Great Splendour' (Ta-Ming), better known as the Ming dynasty.

The Ming period produced little during the first hundred years that was new in painting, and the great Yüan style, directly connected with the Sung, continued to flourish.

Apart from the Emperor Hsüan-tsung (1398-1435) who took the name of Hsüan-tê and was a pleasing painter of bamboo, the first outstanding artist was Tai Chin. In fact he proved one of the most brilliant of Ming artists but, irked by the preference given to literati over painters, he rebelled, was disgraced, withdrew from the court and returned to his native land. During his lifetime he had little success professionally, but after his death his pictures were universally appreciated and he was acclaimed as the founder of a new school of landscapists, the Chê school, from Chekiang, the name of the region where he was born. There is a considerable variance of style in the two periods of his career. The picture *Returning Home at Evening in Spring* (Plate 49), attributed to him, clearly shows his debt to the Yüan masters. The trees stand out clearly against the luminous atmosphere of twilight just as Ma Lin might have treated them, and the use of the 'dry brush' is a trick of the sensitive Ni Tsan. During his voluntary exile, however, Tai Chin used his sensitive brush-stroke and line in a very different way, and in rapidly descriptive compositions he gained new experience in various fields, including bamboo painting. The balance he achieved between line, modelling and colour gives all his work the greatest of validity and originality. He was the type of man who could not give of his best when commissioned or forced by others to submit to discipline, and in this too lies his greatness.

About the end of the 15th century or the beginning of the 16th, there came into being a school formed by a group of artists living in or near Su-chou in the Wu district, in the Yangtze river delta. Known as the Wu school, it was to play an important part in the renewal of the literati tradition.

Judging by the way in which the Ming critics spoke of it, one might get a wrong idea, for in this context the word 'school' does not have quite the same meaning as it has in the West. True, the painters living in that particular centre had a certain amount of influence over each other but the grouping was more imaginary than real, suggested by the prevalence of philosophical and religious considerations over those of style. In any case, we can say that one of the essential characteristics of the Wu painters was the harmony of their lives with that of the community in which they lived. Wu painters were not shut up within themselves or in their art as had been many of their Yüan predecessors, who had been wrongly accused of being antisocial. Nor did Wu painters assume the rebellious attitude of their successors in the first Ch'ing period, that of men invincibly hostile to the political world around them. Recently the importance of this has been reassessed but without taking into account the profound reasons for the isolation of the Yüan artists or the rebellion of the last of the Mings. Moreover, one must remember that the ethical and social thinking of those days was far removed from ours. In those times no one would have thought it odd that people, especially peasants, should revolt, eliminate the Mongols, then hasten to restore both state and culture on still narrower traditional lines.

The chief exponents of the Wu school were Shên Chou (1427-1509), who is considered the founder, and Wên Chêng-ming (1470-1599), his pupil. After them came other masters of greater or lesser degree, among them Wên Chêng-ming's son, Wên Chia (1501-1583), and nephew, Wên Po-jên (1502-1580).

53. Wên Chêng-ming (1470-1559). *Philosopher by a Waterfall*. Ming dynasty. National Museum, Stockholm.

54. T'ang Yin (1470-1523). *Fishermen on the River in Autumn*. Ming dynasty. National Palace and Central Museum Collections, Taichung (Taiwan).

53.   Wên Chêng-ming (1470-1559). *Philosopher by a Water-fall.* Ming dynasty. National Museum, Stockholm. A hanging scroll where the application of ink and colour which make up the gorge establish a new way of building a composition of almost modern expressive force.

54.   T'ang Yin (1470-1523). *Fishermen on the River in Autumn.* Ming dynasty. National Palace and Central Museum Collections, Taichung (Taiwan). Hand scroll in ink and colour on silk. An ordinary scene, but relived by the alert mind of the artist, a scene conveying a feeling of profound serenity dominated by the gigantic overhanging rocks.

55

55. Ch'iu Ying (active *c.* 1522-1560). *Farewell to Hsun-yang* (detail). Ming dynasty. W. Rockhill Nelson Gallery of Art, Kansas City. Hand scroll in colour on paper. The stylised treatment of trees and of the relief gives this work a particular stylistic appearance.

56. Tung Ch'i-ch'ang (1555-1636). *Landscape.* From an album of eight pages, dated 1601. Vannotti Collection, Lugano. Accompanying the scene with examples of calligraphy, the artist conjures up a mountain landscape by the use of soft colours shaded in, by the archaic stylisation of the mountains, and by altering the proportions, but the result is one of rare evocative power.

56. Tung Ch'i-ch'ang (1555-1636). *Landscape.*
From an album of eight pages, dated 1601.
Vannotti Collection, Lugano.

The extraordinary fame of Shên Chou in his life-time was due first and foremost to his being one of the most brilliant of the literati. No doubt Wên Chêng-ming exaggerated in calling him one of the Immortals, yet Shên Chou was always a skilful painter even when he imitated Ni Tsan and Wang Mêng, and he had a very personal style which, according to various critics was better suited to the hand scroll than the hanging scroll. In his 'vertical' landscapes the steep slope of the earth, the heavy masses on top and the whimsical perspective sometimes make it seem as though the most distant masses are about to slip down on to the foreground, a not unpleasing, if illogical, effect.

Wên Chêng-ming, Shên Chou's pupil, was more varied in his compositions, and the wider range of his brush-strokes earned his style the definition 'fastidi-ous'. This characteristic is particularly evident in the hanging scroll dated 1531 and entitled *Pines and Cypresses by the Waterfall*. In *The Farewell,* dated 1524, Wên Chêng-ming puts two slender little figures be-side a clump of trees, indifferent yet oppressive like a cluster of sad memories.

Partially connected with the Wu school was T'ang Yin (1470-1523), a painter whose tormented life, end-ing in unjust condemnation, is reflected in his style and pictures. There is nothing in them reminiscent of the Yüan period, but sometimes in the construction of the rocks, he uses the angular brush-strokes of Li T'ang, a Sung painter who specialised in animals.

Ch'iu Ying's only connection with the Wu school was that he had worked in Su-chou and derived some details of style from the two great masters. He was, in fact, the only professional painter among so many literati, and this alone, according to the canons of the literati style, sufficed to dissociate him from the school. But his genius was unanimously recognised and he was welcomed in artistic circles at Su-chou. The critics praised him, thus ensuring his immediate success.

Unfortunately his name suffers today through the many copies and poor derivations attributed to him by unscrupulous dealers.

Those Ming critics and, to some extent, their successors made use of the experiences of the Wu school and its offshoots with the result that the school itself had an influence upon both the formation of the successive painters and the evaluation of their work. It was as though a solid base had been formed on which there was no place for evolution except of a secondary nature—the diminished importance of the 'flowers and birds' motif, for example, or the greater interest in bamboos or new symbolic values such as those attributed to the flowering plum, the chrysanthemum and the orchid. This base had great weight in the evaluation of works of the past as well, and to detach himself from it a critic needed a strong personality and real genius. It is easy for us to see that, though there were reactions, they were never total or revolutionary. Nevertheless a heterogeneous group was formed, the 'nine painter friends'.

The chief of these was Tung Ch'i-ch'ang (1555-1636). Like his friend and colleague, Mo Shih-lung (active 1567-1582), he was also a writer and an art critic. Among other things, he renewed interest in technical problems, a matter to which people were devoting much time outside the artistic world as well. From the study of the ancient masters, he said, what was to be gleaned was not their forms or technique but only an understanding of their *'ch'i yün'*, the untranslatable essence to which the first of the Six Principles referred. Judging by the pictures which he painted in the style of various artists of the past, it seems that he showed, even in copies, nothing but his own personality and his own inspiration. His *Landscape* (Plate 56) is an example of this. It is inspired by Ni Tsan but Tung Ch'i-ch'ang expresses that master's spirit with an entirely different technique and, especially in the force with which the mountains seem to come out from the bosom of the earth, ends up by creating a composition far removed from anything that Ni Tsan would have painted.

As unlike Tung Ch'i-ch'ang as could be, Ch'ên Hung-shou put his archaic style at the service of a pronounced predilection for the bizarre. Wang Chien (1598-1677) and Wang Shih-min (1592-1680) were also friends of Tung Ch'i-ch'ang but they really belonged to the Ch'ing period.

57

57.   Wang Chien (1598-1677). *Mountain Landscape.* Ch'ing dynasty. Freer Gallery of Art, Washington. Hanging scroll in ink and light colour on paper. This is a composition on classic lines which, although inspired by the landscapes of Wang Mêng, differs from them considerably in its minute attention to detail and a clarity greater than that of the traditional view.

58.   Chu Ta, called Pa-ta Shan-jên (1626-*c.* 1705). *Mountain Landscape.* Ch'ing dynasty. Academy of Arts, Honolulu. Detail of an album leaf in ink and colour on silk.

59.   Chu Ta, called Pa-ta Shan-jên (1626-*c.* 1705). *River Landscape.* Academy of Arts, Honolulu. Album leaf in ink and light colour on silk. In this and the preceding Plate one can see how the painter's very personal style triumphs. It embraces line and relief, stylisations and delicate realistic details, all of which go to make his interpretation of nature singularly effective. By being divorced from total reality, the work of this Buddhist monk has a very modern look, one readily appreciated by Western eyes.

60.   Fang Shih-shu (1692-1751). *Landscape.* Ch'ing dynasty. Staatliche Museen, Berlin. A bright picture dominated by clear perspective achieved through technical skill in the composition. The influence of Chu Ta's brush-work is especially evident in Fang Shih-shu's rendering of the trees and in the accurate details in the foreground.

58. Chu Ta, called Pa-ta Shan-jên (1626-*c.* 1705). *Mountain Landscape.* Ch'ing dynasty. Academy of Arts, Honolulu.

59. Chu Ta, called Pa-ta Shan-jên (1626-*c.* 1705). *River Landscape*. Academy of Arts, Honolulu.

60. Fang Shih-shu (1692-1751). *Landscape*. Ch'ing
dynasty. Staatliche Museen, Berlin.

Preceded by another economic crisis, the Ming period came to an end with the rapid rise of a rebel peasant who occupied Peking and forced the last emperor to commit suicide. On this occasion, however, the educated class preferred to ask foreigners to help them resolve the situation. General Wu San-kuei, who had been fighting the Manchus, turned about and, uniting traditional enemies under his command, reconquered Peking (1644), but he could not prevent the barbarians declaring their young sovereign, Shun-chih, legitimate heir to the throne. Naturally, not everybody accepted the *fait accompli*. Of the artists, at least three faced death for their loyalty to the now deposed dynasty. They were Ni Yuang-lu (1593-1644), Yang Wên-ts'ung (1597-1645), and Huang Tao-chou (1585-1646). Rather than submit to the foreigners, many others lived in retirement, but remained rebels at heart. They were the great 'individualists'. With their eccentric bearing, their most unusual sort of life and the unquestionable originality of their talent, they imposed themselves upon the entire country. The chief, or one of the greatest, of them was Chu Ta (1626-*c*. 1705), the painter who chose to remain without speaking for a long period of his life. Better known as Pa-ta Shan-jên, a descendant of the imperial Ming family, he became a Buddhist monk, and, it is said, took to drink and suffered from delirium tremens. But this did not prevent his creating works of exceptional vigour. Though lightly traced, his brush-work is firm and aggressive. At times, his men and women are slightly ill-placed or out of balance, but, with horizontal foliage on the trees, vertical lines on the mountains, hooked brush-strokes curving back on themselves for the masses, his landscapes rank among the finest expressions of the Chinese genius. With his brush, he could obtain most impressive effects of perspective and relief.

Following the path that he trod, though with more balance, came Ch'a Shih-piao (1615-1698). At the fall of the Ming dynasty, he retired from public employment, lived apart and dedicated himself to his art, becoming the chief of a group of painters known as the Four Masters of Anhwei (the next most important member was Hung-jên, who had become a Buddhist monk when barely twenty to escape from the Ch'ings). Ch'a Shih-piao's style has Ni Tsan's 'dry brush' and, above all, the sense of solitude which dominates his landscapes. Ni Tsan was also the source of inspiration from time to time for the highly cultured Wu Li (1632-c. 1718), poet, talented musician and the last great painter of flowers. He was a Taoist, but was converted to Catholicism at the age of fifty and became a Jesuit. As a painter, however, he remained deeply attached to the Chinese tradition. So much so, in fact, that, as noted earlier, he accused European painting of being made of light and shadow. Associated by the critics of his day with the 'Four Wangs' until, with Yün Shou-p'ing, he formed the so-called 'Six Ch'ing

61. Ch'a Shih-piao (1615-1698). *Crossing a Mountain River on a Donkey.* Hanging scroll dated 1678. Ch'ing dynasty. Dubosc Collection, Lugano.

62. Wu Li (1632-*c.* 1718). *Landscape in the style of Ni Tsan*. Ch'ing dynasty. Vannotti Collection, Lugano.

63. Wang Chien (1598-1677). *Landscape.*
Hanging scroll signed and dated 1666. Ch'ing
dynasty. Vannotti Collection, Lugano.

61. Ch'a Shih-piao (1615-1698). *Crossing a Mountain River on a Donkey.* Ch'ing dynasty. Dubosc Collection, Lugano. Hanging scroll in ink and colour on silk dated 1678. A fine work in which contemporary experience comes to the service of a classicising sensibility in the search for harmonious composition.

62. Wu Li (1632-*c.* 1718). *Landscape in the style of Ni Tsan.* Ch'ing dynasty. Vannotti Collection, Lugano. Hanging scroll in ink and a very light colour-wash on paper, signed with the pseudonym (*tzu*) Mo-ching. The calm meditated uncoloured tradition of Ni Tsan lives again in the work of Wu Li showing the persistence of values badly interpreted by Western critics. They saw nothing but a negative evaluation in the Chinese critics' judgment of Ni Tsan's painting as 'flat and uncoloured'.

63. Wang Chien (1598-1677). *Landscape.* Ch'ing dynasty. Vannotti Collection, Lugano. Hanging scroll painted in ink and a light colour-wash, signed and dated 1666. According to the author's inscription it was inspired by the style of Huang Kung-wang, painter and critic of the Yüan period, a style which, though more balanced, was the prelude to the unorthodox style of Chu Ta and his contemporaries.

64. Wang Shih-min (1592-1680). *Landscape.* Ch'ing dynasty. Vannotti Collection, Lugano. Hanging scroll in ink on paper, signed and dated 1647. This picture also, according to the inscription of the author, was inspired by Huang Kung-wang's style, but here the resemblance is clearly much greater.

丁亥夏日倣大癡
華亭 王時敏

64

135

65

65. Wang Hui (1632-1717). *Landscape.* Ch'ing
dynasty. Vannotti Collection, Lugano.

66. Wang Hui (1632-1717). *Landscape.* Ch'ing dynasty.
Vannotti Collection, Lugano.

66

65.   Wang Hui (1632-1717). *Landscape.* Ch'ing dynasty. Vannotti Collection, Lugano. Hand scroll in ink and colour on paper. This classical composition was inspired, as the inscription states, by Kuan T'ung (end of the 9th century or the beginning of the 10th), and the massive structure of the mountain is derived from him.

66.   Wang Hui (1632-1717). *Landscape.* Ch'ing dynasty. Vannotti Collection, Lugano. Album leaf in ink and light colour on paper. This landscape, centred chiefly on the towering twisted mountain, is certainly one of the best works in the whole of Wang Hui's vast production.

67

67. Kung Hsien (active *c.* 1660-1700). *Landscape.* Ch'ing dynasty. W. Rockhill Nelson Gallery of Art, Kansas City. Detail of a hand scroll in ink·on paper. Kung Hsien is one of the great 'individualists'. That he was an innovator appears clearly in this work. Its tiny brush-strokes make the masses seem covered with windswept grass.

Masters', he stood out from them with his skill and creative independence. But this did not prevent his having been a pupil of Wang Shih-min and a friend of Wang Hui, the greatest of the Four Wangs.

The oldest of the Four Wangs was Wang Shih-min (1592-1680) and he had been a pupil of Tung Ch'i-ch'ang. He handled his brush well and evolved new strokes but basically he was arid although, in the opinion of his contemporaries, his virtuosity placed him far above the dull painters of the imperial academy which the increasing interest in art and its technique did not succeed in reviving. There was also another Wang, Wang Chien (1598-1677) and, oddly enough, the work of the one was often difficult to distinguish from that of the other. In the treatises on painting, these first two Wangs were called 'the first generation'.

For his ability to synthesise and his wide eclectic experience, the greatest of the group was undoubtedly Wang Hui (1632-1717). He had a long and active career, and his favourite saying was, 'The best painting cannot be based on [the study of] a particular master or [of] a particular school.' Although less gifted than his uncle and teacher, Wang Hui's nephew, Wang Yüan-ch'i (1642-1715) gained important posts and honours.

But the one great artist of the Ch'ing period was Kung Hsien (active 1656-1682). In him technical perfection walked hand-in-hand with carefully balanced composition and elegant use of ink and colour. In his landscapes there is seldom room for the human figure, however tiny. All is dominated by a sense of mystery and, in spite of the rich vegetation, the ghostliness of moonlight. This reveals a meditative spirit fascinated by the immensity of nature, yet, for all his absorption, Kung Hsien does not miss its cruel indifference when autumn turns to winter. Like all Chinese art critics, eager to group painters of a particular period into little series, later writers put him at the head of a group called the 'Eight Masters of Chin-ling' (modern Nanking), flanking him with other painters who happened to live there in the second half of the 17th century. The writers formed the group haphazardly, taking no account of styles; but in any case Kung Hsien's powerful style and technique earned him not only immediate fame but also the right to be placed at the head of the group as the greatest exponent of the Nanking school and, more generally, of 17th-century China.

To complete this brief account of the Ch'ing painters let us recall the 'Two Stones', two good painters coupled by a play on words. The first was K'un-ts'an (active *c.* 1650-1675), professionally known as Shih-ch'i. The second was Tao-chi (1630-1707), also known as Shih-t'ao. Because 'Shih' means 'a stone', the pair were known as the Two Stones even in contemporary treatises. K'uan-ts'an was one of the 'individualists' and withdrew from the world because

68. Kung Hsien. *Landscape with Bridge*

68. Kung Hsien (active *c.* 1660-1700). *Landscape with Bridge.* Ch'ing dynasty. Vannotti Collection, Lugano. Album leaf in ink on paper, dated 1684. The entangled vegetation along the river is seen by the painter as impressionistic foliage caressed by the wind.

69. Tao-chi (1630-1707). Illustration for an episode of the tale by T'ao Yuan-ming, *The Peach Blossom Spring.* Ch'ing dynasty. Freer Gallery of Art, Washington. Hand scroll in ink and light colour on paper. Tao-chi's style and thought fuse miraculously in this composition which tells of refugees fleeing from tyranny to an imaginary valley. With winding lines the painter evokes mountains and precipices. The 'simple brush-stroke', short and precise, serves for men, houses, distant trees.

70. Tao-chi (1630-1707). *Landscape.* Ch'ing dynasty. Vannotti Collection, Lugano. Album leaf in ink and light colours on paper. The stylisation of some of the trees contrasts with the realistic mountain peaks lightly clad in mist.

71. Hung-jên (*c.* 1603-1663). *Landscape.* Ch'ing dynasty. Vannotti Collection, Lugano. One of the twelve pages of an album in ink and light colour, dated 1656. Note the hazy mountains in the distance and the stylised trees standing out in relief.

69. Tao-chi (1630-1707). Illustration for an episode
of the tale by T'ao Yuan-ming, *The Peach Blossom Spring*.
Ch'ing dynasty. Freer Gallery of Art, Washington.

70. Tao-chi (1630-1707). *Landscape*. Ch'ing dynasty.
Vannotti Collection, Lugano.

蓬芳已似
雄麗我
風月誰同
共一朝好
水好山看
獸足但存
曾鹿敢云
饒

71. Hung-jên (*c.* 1603-1663). *Landscape.* Ch'ing dynasty.
Vannotti Collection, Lugano.

he had a true religious vocation. Alone with nature, he sought not only truth but that instant of light in which a landscape reveals its essence. Then, without pausing, his minute brush-strokes painted the details, graduating their clarity and visibility according to distance and light. Without drawing long shadows, the brush succeeds perfectly in capturing that second which separates twilight from the start of darkness in the rapid Chinese sunset. Tao-chi's brush was slightly slower. When asked whether he belonged to the northern or southern school, he used to laugh and say: 'I paint in my own style.' When asked about method, he said his was a 'non-method'. With those very long brush-strokes drawing mountains and valleys at times right back through the scene, at others defining the limits, Tao-chi is perhaps nearer our modern style. He twists and curls as though he were making some monstrous diagram illustrating the pulse of geological life.

The last of the Ch'ing artists of more than ordinary quality was Lo P'ing (1733-1799). His capacity for mocking the masters of old and indulging in calculated distortion has led to his valuation in the West. His impossible rocks reduced almost to pieces of modern sculpture repeat an effect favoured by Wang Meng and other painters but they do it in a fantastic manner.

For the whole of the 19th century, Chinese painting looked back at what it used to be, becoming nothing more than a nostalgic evocation of a glorious past. Only after the Sino-Japanese War of 1894-1895 were there signs of a growing interest in European and Europeanised Japanese techniques. Perspective, nudes, drapery, chiaroscuro, all these were closely studied, and French painting acquired an unrivalled prestige.

Nevertheless the two great masters who dominated Chinese painting in the first half of the 20th century both follow traditional techniques though each strove after different effects.

Known almost exclusively by his Europeanised surname, Jupéon, Hsu Pei-hung (1894-1957) became famous for his horses although their excessive repetition in every possible manner ended up in their becoming a sort of decoration. In fact, that is just how they are used in the West, and the reproductions are not always of high standard. Jupéon's style derived from Ch'an painting although he used his ink more descriptively and, in a certain sense, gave it more movement.

Less known than Jupéon but more gifted with expressive powers, Ch'i Pai-shih (1860-1957) is the last great painter in modern times. During the last fifteen years much study has been devoted to the Tun-huang murals, Western techniques have been adopted and adapted with taste to Chinese needs. The leading representative of traditional tendencies and the courageous revivalist of Yüan and Ming trends is the

72. Tai Pen Hsiao (1621-1691). *Fantastic Landscape.* Ch'ing dynasty. Vannotti Collection, Lugano.

73

72.   Tai Pen Hsiao (1621-1691). *Fantastic Landscape.* Ch'ing dynasty. Vannotti Collection, Lugano. Hanging scroll in ink and light colour on paper. Mountains, twisted and smooth like great splinters of rock, overhang a half-hidden house dominated by a pine-tree in a clever play of volumes.

73.   Lo P'ing (1733-1799). *Orchids and Rocks.* Ch'ing dynasty. Vannotti Collection, Lugano. Hanging scroll in ink on paper, with long text. Pierced like a sponge, the distorted monstrous rock reveals the skill and style of this artist which have been fully re-evaluated recently by Western critics.

74.   Kao Ch'i-p'ei (*c.* 1672-1734). *Landscape with Towering Peaks.* Ch'ing dynasty. Rijksmuseum, Amsterdam. Album leaf in ink and colour on paper. The inscription is particularly striking. The ink was applied not only with a brush but with the fingers and nails as well. Kao let one of his nails grow and used it, notched at the tip, to obtain effects which he could not get with his brush.

famous woman painter, Tseng Yu-ho. On the other hand, Marxist trends have developed book illustration and wood-cuts, and the vigorous quality of the work produced far exceeds their value as propaganda for which they are primarily intended.

74. Kao Ch'i-p'ei (*c.* 1672-1734). *Landscape with Towering Peaks.* Ch'ing dynasty. Rijksmuseum, Amsterdam.

LIST OF ILLUSTRATIONS

Page